# LIGHTS & MYSTERIES

# LIGHTS & MYSTERIES

ເຈ

THOMAS CENTOLELLA

COPPER CANYON PRESS

Publication of this book is supported by a grant from the National Endowment
for the Arts and a grant from the Lannan Foundation. Additional support to Cop-
per Canyon Press has been provided by the Andrew W. Mellon Foundation, the
Lila Wallace–Reader's Digest Fund, and the Washington State Arts Commission.
Copper Canyon Press is in residence with Centrum at Fort Worden State Park.

Library of Congress Cataloging-in-Publication Data
Centolella, Thomas
Lights and mysteries : poems / by Thomas Centolella.
p.   cm.
ISBN 1-55659-106-3 (pbk.)
1. Title.
PS3553.E65L54 1995
811'.54 – dc20                 95-32542

COPPER CANYON PRESS
P.O. BOX 271, PORT TOWNSEND, WASHINGTON 98368

## ACKNOWLEDGMENTS

My gratitude to the editors of the following publications where some of these poems were first printed: *Ploughshares, Hayden's Ferry Review, Collecting Moon Coins, Vol. II,* and *Alaska Quarterly Review.*

Deep thanks to Sam Hamill, Denise Levertov, Carl Dennis, and my students at College of Marin for their vital and abiding interest.

Profound appreciation to Jeanie Kim, Kate Moses, and the Lannan Foundation, whose magnanimity was not only timely but exemplified the highest standard for the encouragement of writers.

And love to my family and my friends, my fellow "cosmic travelers." Further in, further on.

*For Madre & Padre*

# CONTENTS

I.

II.

III.

# LIGHTS & MYSTERIES

I.

I exist because I have loved you,
Beauty so ancient and so new.
I exist because I have loved you.

    — *St. Augustine*

## PROVENANCE

We were talking our way through the source
of great art, of great lives, and suffering
seemed the least of it. The back road dark,
half-moon obscured by the slowest clouds.
In the flesh of my hand lay the knowledge
of her flesh: it seemed both true and beautiful,
not all I knew on earth, but all I needed
to know. We walked the long slow walk
that would lead, thrillingly, back to each other,
and regarded Van Gogh as the religious impulse
taken to its logical conclusion: spirit and matter
suffused: a still life, a landscape, a self-
portrait so loved he laid on the paint, gladly
possessed by what he saw, given to his vision,
determined to ensure it with the mystical
three dimensions. Someone who could say, "I know
well enough what I want. I am indifferent
to criticism…" – and live it so well
that many years later I would come to
these sunflowers the years haven't touched,
and ache to touch them, the everyday immortal ache
of spirit for matter, of matter for spirit:
the same need between us I came to grasp
not only through her hands and lips and voice
but through her eyes: through her unwavering vision
that we could touch what we loved, could hold it,
and, beheld, it would last.

How wise we thought our bodies were
to turn off the road to the immortal
and give the everyday a chance.
The river that gave us a long green light.
A garden walled with wild rose.
My white summer shirt, her straw-hat with holes,
a four-poster anywhere. The hyper innkeeper,
hurrying to an emergency, who blurted out,
"I'll be back when I can – *you* are the innkeepers!"
leaving us with her five-year-old grandson
and his German shepherd: with what preternatural calm
the dog lay on its paws while boy surgeon
applied to its tail his blue toy saw.
After the day went away the bug-lights crackled
with blue death – which only briefly reminded us
of our own short stay. Then it was back to the room
she said she never wanted to leave, back to action
taken on impulse, and the stillness just before.
In the perilous world, in the world that moved
too fast for its own good, our bodies performed
a remarkable feat: they slowed. They lingered.
They looked for the fork in the road
that told us we were almost home.
No matter how far we drifted, our bodies knew
to circle back, like beggars to the temple
where they'd been given something more than a taste.
Even as equivocation raised its tiresome voice,
speaking first one mind, then the other, our bodies knew
to dig right in and eat with the fingers:
what carries us has a mind of its own
and rarely stands on ceremony. Our bodies
made certain we'd arrive safely, and later enjoy
the night's accommodations. And that waking up

would be the order of the day. Every day
I learned to take what was given freely,
abiding appetite, not-to-be-denied appetite,
which is the body's way. And every night
I learned to welcome the secret, scented offerings
made without sacrifice, for which we felt almost guilty,
so much easy grace had come back to our bodies.
In an overgrown field of ancient headstones
the sun never felt so good. "Is it true?" she asked.
"Do we really have to die?" Yes, no – what did it matter?
Every world we knew, the one long gone, the one
still going, depended on our simplest gesture.
Those weren't high winds that rattled the bedroom windows,
that swirled the chimes drunkenly above the porch –
those were ghosts, famished, clamoring for more.

The day had not been created yet.
White fog into which the streetcars vanished.
I said: Behind this emptiness there's a brightness.
She said: I like that. At Ocean Beach

the sun came out like a host greeting the new guests.
I loved the sleek dogs in heat, and the ones that chased them,
their fluid shifts in direction, their sudden stops –
nose to ass – then off again. She loved the *basso* rumble

of water rolling, the one sand dollar
undiminished, green glass passing for emeralds,
and a curl of a shell, pearly white,
she identified at once as an angel's wing.

I loved the headlands in mist, the swirl
of current around my ankles, that icy sting,
the gold cliff crowned by cypresses
hard wind had made to lean landward.

She loved the heavy ropes of sea kelp,
the late clouds – pinkish delicacies – the graffitied
sea wall, where an Assyrian horse in full gallop
hovered in place. And me, she loved me.

And I loved her. That much was clear.
It didn't mean a life together.
Or it did, but in a way yet to be created.
I fit my spine into a dune like part of the dune

while she went back to combing the beach.
Closed my eyes, glad to give myself
to what's always there, what never dies.
And more than glad to be received.

That's what she said the night it was evident
all that had been ours might come to nothing.
This was long after our state-of-the-cosmos conversation
by starlight, under redwoods, kindred spirits on a cold night.
This was after the first kiss and the second thoughts,
the gift of Hungarian glass like a wafer of blue ice
and a water pitcher blue as a robin's egg, the paper narcissus
crisp and erect. This was well after the wild secret
that would remain a secret, and the fatal mistake, and the unexpected
child who would not be born. This was after a four-year-old
in a white dress materialized out of the evening air,
and with great ceremony entrusted her "magic seeds" to our open
    palms.
This was long after July's annual light show
paled next to our pyrotechnics, and Independence Day
arrived more than once that year...


                                    And then, on the night
of longest hours: *Tell me again about the sacred.*
Like someone dying, like someone being abducted
to the underworld and asking for courage.
What could I say that hadn't been said already
and said in the most splendid way: in simple words
no one would forget as long as they lived;
and then without words, simply through the rhythm
of splendid day becoming night becoming day. Perfect
presents had been exchanged, according to the custom,
not a few invisible to the jaded eye, and beneath
the striking surfaces, the ingenious effects,
curled up in its powers, timeless, benign, the sacred slept.

Of course, it was our sleep. We were like the stillborn,
the soul suspended too far from the body's reach.

If only the sacred would speak for itself.
But it was forcing us to rouse it
the way you'd wake a child: a hand smoothing back
the hair, a whisper in the ear, a kiss on the cheek.
What would be until then only dream
would lead to the real, though no less rich or wild.
She wanted, she said, to be protected from the world.
I wanted to wake her to it – the way any of us,
after a long night of wandering among the perished
and the lost and the doomed, will open our eyes,
and there, once again: the warm, the familiar, the cherished.

## ADORATION

It was Sunday, day of the bright sun,
the warped dock, the wet dog by a small lake.
Day of improbable names: Angels Camp,
Love Creek Road. The water a forest green
except in shadow near the far shore
where it was nearly frozen. The December air
mild for the season, and the sky an ultra blue
from which would fall, not snow, or even rain,
but apples. The last apples of the year, many
still unnamed, many the color of a high ardor,
scarlet and golden, blush and flame, and all against the winter
gray of branches, like Christmas ornaments on a tree
more beautiful for having been stripped of its greenery.
The mountain sky perfectly blue, and a great heron less blue
but no less perfect, that rose from a gleam of reeds
to glide not a yard above the water, and light
in the topmost limb of a pine. I looked over at the one
who meant the world to me, and said,
"Now if that isn't a sign…" And she agreed:
Good fortune would be ours.

She wanted to reach the little snow
that lay on the far shore in patches –
"We have to touch that" is how she put it –
and we followed the bear scat that ringed the lake
until we were there. I lobbed a hefty rock
that punctured the ice with a clean *ka-thunk,*
and she fired off a few stones that went skidding
with a *ping ping ping,* a surprise of electronic tones
that resonated through the glen. We had discovered
again, and without even trying, the art
of play: we played the lake
as if it were the most ancient instrument.

We invented a ritual that was laughable,
anointing each other's cheeks
with snow. And every time I held her
tightly, expecting the air to be a little colder,
the light scarcer, the time to say goodbye at hand,
time itself joined in and played against my expectations:
it left us alone. Standing there that close,
it could have been one long life together
come down to one long day. Or one moment
that was nothing if not life itself.

Already in our part of the world, the obsession
for giving presents had returned, a gesture
begun in adoration by the wise
thousands of years before. The hard year
had come round to giving again, to the replenishment
of the poor, and the poor of spirit, to the thought
(though we could hardly bear it) that every year brought
its squandering of riches, and the new year
might be as rough. On a hard patch of earth
we found our cold arms full of each other
and nothing left to give – each of us the gift
we would have to keep for ourselves,
and learn to accept as enough.

I've seen them all over the city. After midnight
near the consulate, closer to the streetlight
than you might expect: a parked car, windows misted,
wings for a trademark. And the muffled urgencies
from the back seat – someone about to die, perhaps,
or be delivered – the sleek silhouette of a woman's legs
lifted and spread behind the fogged glass,
and between her legs, a slow moving, a denser kind
of fog… Or outside the bus terminal late in the day,
at commuter peak, the sedan that sat illicitly
by the crosswalk, the jowly man in the driver's seat
going nowhere for now: head back, eyes closed, mouth
open like a slaughtered pig's, while his companion worked
her blonde head over his lap, and a thousand people off work
too intent on getting home even to notice.

But we never took that route, that strange craving
to be caught in the act, have others confirm our willingness
to trust reasons that reason itself could never explain.
When she came to me it was for moments
she couldn't claim well enough on her own to keep,
and I took her to where the world endured, the elements
held sway. The small town a temblor had ruined,
blocks of exposed foundations that went deep.
A houseboat where, twice a day, high tide kept us buoyant.
And the coastal road with its blind turns that ended in air
and dared us to keep going, to live that vista.
Whatever we were looking for seemed to find us,
and the only ones to bear witness were a solitary
egret, a yellow moon, the stripped-naked limbs of eucalyptus.

And once, off a high trail, after a warm rain,
her face gleaming, eyes intent, nipples showing

through her soaked blouse, she pressed me against a tree,
said, "I like holding it in my hand," before she took me
into her mouth, one rapt creature at fullest power, feeding
on another. And the pale mountain flowers, barely-there
pinks and blues, like colors for the unborn children
we'd only dream about – these are what she drew
all over her letters later, like another language
altogether, as if words alone couldn't be trusted,
couldn't do justice to that kind of need.
While above us that day, as above us now, lazing
on their massive, recurring thermals: the raptors,
seemingly at play, but raking the valley floor
for anything alive and there for the taking,
anything worth killing for.

EVENSONG

I could have gone this evening to evensong.
Watched the light from a star on its way to dust
arrive at my cathedral's nave, collaborate
with colored glass, and dazzle the congregation.
But it's all paled for me, the luminous, the legendary
lives of saints (alleged to be as human as us
but impossibly strong). And my idea of exaltation?
A grunting old woman with grocery bags, her own joints
nearly leaden, trudging in from the street
not so much to be delivered from evil
as to get out of the cold and off her swollen feet.

I could have gone to evensong and joined the singers
from my choice seat near the sanctuary,
in that pew where another woman (exempt from pain
because much younger, one of fate's loveliest chosen few)
let my long fingers stroke her long fingers,
and settled her fragrant head on my shoulder
in full view of the bishop – whose smile,
though benign as a saint's, was a far cry
from laughter, as if we embodied the kingdom
and the power and the glory
he had always hungered after.

No surprise that I go to evensong anyway
when I close my eyes. I go out of spite, and irk the mild clergy
with my black leather jacket and the godless smirk
that says faith is for suckers – one of the Dark Prince's
minions, now that I have fallen further
than I ever intended... But above a steady pilot light
fragrant herbs are steeping to balance my humors
(she used to joke I resembled a medieval saint),
and when did I ever feel completely at home

among the cynical one-note gloom-and-doomers?
And the voices I hear when I'm this alone

(somewhere between a locked ward
and a choir primed for heaven)
make their own kind of music
in their own sweet time,
and keep me even.

Morning, the way mornings used to be
before those brilliant few days
when light would stir our sleeping bodies
like revelation. Early morning, the rooms
in half-tones, and I'm holding in my left hand
as if it were some kind of evidence
my own heart: encased in a pouch
of the latest plastic, murky in its own
dark blood: the art of preservation.
Those fine yellow words
from the manufacturer – are they instructions
or a warning? How calm I've become,
pale in the bathroom mirror, a casualty
that by all rights should not even be
breathing, much less on my feet.
On my left side there's the slender bruise,
reddish purple, where my heart (to be replaced?
transplanted?) was deftly removed. Obviously
the operation is incomplete. What I need to do
is reinsert it – it's getting late,
I've got to get to work. I keep thinking:
This is a dream, it ought to be easy,
it should slip right back in-between my ribs…
And wonder to behold, it does.
Then the alarm goes off: it's morning,
time again to go to work. I check my side
in the bathroom mirror: I'm fine,
more or less. Just a little scar
like expensive silk. Just a little tenderness.

She was underneath me. I had my hands on her face.
Sunday morning, in a house surrounded by water.
I stroked that rich color you don't find every day.
Her hair, red and wild, more red, more wild
against the white sheet. The whole place white
but not cold, green hill out the window,
the water gray on its way to silver. We moved
ever so slightly. The house on its moorings creaked.
A little music from her throat, or was it coming
from the bay? We were any two creatures floating.
Wetness everywhere, the whole world liquescent, delicious.
In a white room without time, we were tensed together
without need of time, my hands, my long hands on her face,
the heat there so familiar. Is this prayer, I wanted to know.
And she said, Yes, it is. Make it last forever.

If art's a private religion then so's love.
A couch, a book, a church of two –
there was nothing we didn't take to heart.
Our passions, our imperfections – preparation
for the great life. Beauty so ancient and so new,
and each of us chosen to play a part.

Even now, when *was* means *then*
and not now, not ever again,
I'll find myself reaching for that book,
those soul-deep lines like a proposal
of marriage, and I'll marvel at how much nothing
can come from a singular moment.

Or, in one of my trances, I'll be drifting by the cathedral
where we stood in the sanctuary as if we owned it,
and she dreamed at the ceiling, certain
there was a soul waiting for us to bring it down
into this world of beautiful chances –
and it's the soiled bedroll by the bronze doors I'll notice,

the deadpan eyes of gargoyles, the tourists worshiping
with their viewfinders and automatic focus.
In the end she said, "But if you had it all to do again – "
And I said, "I wouldn't." …Laid out on my white couch
I'm quiet as a crusader in his marble tomb.
No one calls or writes. No one visits,

no one comes to say, "You exist
as you've always existed."
And yet it's true: I exist

because I have loved you,
Beauty so ancient and so new.
I exist because I have loved you.

II.

Alas! the world is full of enormous lights
and mysteries, and man shuts them from himself
with one small hand.

  – *Baal Shem Tov*

# LIGHTS AND MYSTERIES

1.

First thing in the morning, doorbell rings.
Two sharp-looking men in dark suits.
My first thought: FBI. Second thought: Jehovah's
jazz men. And sure enough, the older one almost sings:
"Good morning, sir, how are you this morning?
Can I ask you, sir, if you've thought about why
the world has turned to so much calamity,
and what we should turn to in this awful time?"

"Well," I say, "that's a pretty tall order
on such short notice" – and I look him in the eye –
"especially first thing in the morning.
But I do think about it, every day."
Which, after all, is not exactly a lie. *Uh huh,*
*uh huh,* go their nodding heads, like session men
not only in the same key but on the same wavelength,
and it's gonna be one heavenly jam.

Then the younger one slips from his satchel
the pamphlets of apocalypse, and I offer
a polite no thanks, closing the door
before they can show me the sure way
to salvation, wishing them what they came for,
what all of us are here for in good faith
and trepidation: a nice day.

2.

The first thing in the morning I used to hear
was the *clang bang brang* of a construction crew
laying a foundation for the next generation

of working poor. The gang, barely out of high school,
would rather shout than speak – all the usual
four-letter words and a couple of choice five-letter ones –
and once, when they took their lunch break
not ten feet from the living room
where I was trying to make a living
over the glass-rattling din of an x-rated rap
booming from an arsenal of woofers and tweeters,
I rapped the window my landlady had painted shut,
gave them a "beat it" sign with my thumb,
and got back the snarl of *Are you telling us
or asking us?* Some in headbands, some in ball caps
turned backwards, as though they were court jesters
who lived to contradict the ruling class.
*I'm asking you,* I snarled back, and when
they took their time, inching to the other side
of the site, I summoned a few choice words of my own.

It took months of this, morning after morning
after morning of interrupted sleep – *clang bang brang,
fuck you, suck me, pussy ho' bitch* –
months and months of this, before I slipped
into the reverie of sawed-off shotgun
blasting their oblivious asses into oblivion.

3.

I've heard that the place where you're happiest
is on the way to the place where you believe
you'll be happiest. On my way
to Virginia – which locals say is for lovers,
which lovers say is a refuge, which refugees
must regard as heaven on earth – on my way to Virginia
I walked through my neighborhood in California.
Hanging from the mission church named after the saint

who loved the down-and-out: party-colored pennants,
each bright inverted triangle a hieroglyph
for "festival." I'd forgotten all about these flags
from the days I hadn't yet reached the age
when you're able, says the Church, to distinguish
good from evil. Pennants strung like motley teeth
along the mission's little white stucco wall
where chatty tourists smile for posterity,
while on the other side the native dead lie nameless
beneath the commemorated who murdered them,
and all lie under the hush of a snapshot garden.
I remembered the Vermont graveyard from the summer before:
one headstone like a dark mirror, the epitaph
in rhyming couplets alluding to "monster Death,"
how we stood in the sun, in the overgrown grass,
the only ones around still breathing, and she said,
without a hint or note of terror, "Is it true?
Do we really have to die?" Her own teeth small
and white, and right then I knew: this was the beginning,
not of romance, but love. This little yard of
graves, the true garden where every love begins.


4.


How could I have forgotten these pennants
like shark-toothed monster Death,
but which hung from the mission soft and harmless,
the fangs of some benign creature: Beast
of the Church Bazaar, of the Holy Feast?

How could I have forgotten the booths of homemade pizza
and sausage loaves and fried dough and lemon ice?
The rides that thrilled you as they threatened
to bring up your dinner in one dizzying wave.
And the ring toss, the *pop* of dart-into-balloon,

the trinkets given as prizes I took for real prizes:
a yellow tin cricket that clicked when you pressed it;
a rubber salamander, fire-eyed, which I kept in my hand
as a shaman would a talisman (though at six
I wouldn't have heard of these exotic words).

I'd forgotten the world could be given to me
without intercession of symbols, preconception
of attitudes, interpretation of facts, declaration
of feelings. The pennants were waving slowly
and it was easy to think they were saying hello
and not goodbye – hello again, it's been too long –

and I thought of the world as a child might:
playground by day, carnival by night,
the day and the night reserving
their most genial secrets
for the pure of heart.

5.

After the twelve-year-old was stolen at knife point from her own bed-
room – her terrified girlfriends (who were to sleep over) tied up and
face down on the floor, pillowcases over their heads, her mother just
down the hall, sleeping soundly – a child so attractive even her grand-
parents would tell the media, "She was such an exceptionally pretty girl,
we always thought something like this might happen" – only three days
after the abduction a friend of mine from the same town, a woman who
knows something herself of what it means to be taken against your will,
taken without warning, never to return as you were, my friend said,
"I hope he kills her fast." Meaning the twelve-year-old's murder was a
foregone conclusion and she hoped the girl wouldn't be tortured first.
Meaning she knew enough to skip the requisite but fruitless deceptions
of hope. And I wondered who was right in the long run: the towns-
people, who wasted no time in setting up a foundation to fund the

search for the girl – confident she'd be found alive and well – or my
friend, who sided with Sartre when he said that the most clear-sided
view of the darkest possible situation is itself an act of optimism?

6.

And after traveling to where happiness had beckoned
in the voice of someone who told me,
"You're my speaking self, you give me
the words for the world," I found myself

back where I began: in a room
too raucous by day for peace of mind,
too quiet by night for comfort. A room
without words, without music or meaning,
where I found myself

wondering what had happened
to good faith, the guileless heart,
the world that had taken each of us in
as one of its own. A world
in which beauty existed

only as we existed. So much so
you couldn't tell us apart.

7.

A world in which pathology
passes for your average day:

no one safe from the gun, the knife,
the pipe bomb, the ambush, the air strike,

or the lethal lie of the smile –

goodwill, affection, beautifully feigned…

What keeps me from condemning others
is my ignorance of their pain.

What keeps me from condoning others
is their ignorance of their pain.

8.

How guileless anyone's heart still is,
how wise to believe purity
is equal to calamity,
I don't know. In the deep gaps
where nothing waits, and inside nothing
pure fear, all I know is

that before you can reach the state
reserved for peace, you have to pass through
your own little world: exhaust fumes, street scams,
door-to-door zealots, adolescent parents,
users of controlled substances out of control,
the nomadic tribes of the mentally ill,
illegal immigrants and their bedsheet draperies,
their windowsills of woebegone plaster saints,
the suspicious and the suspect
and the unsuspecting – pass by the slick and costly
window displays, the captains of industry
dressed to kill, the nine-to-fivers murdered
by duty and routine, the jaded schoolkids
who don't know the half of it –

pass through, pass by them all,

and pass somehow back into

that part of yourself still six years old,
untouched by judgment, resilient
to adversity, ready for awe:

9.

a cotton candy vendor so bent by the gods
he was like a bird, his short spine parallel to the ground;
a dark-eyed woman in a dark burnoose
who could detect good fortune in an empty palm;
and a wheel of nightlights that lifted you
higher than you thought you could bear,
and when it brought you down, did it gently,
let you catch your breath, a moment of calm,

before it lifted you back to an overview
so enormous it took your breath away –
and scared the living daylights out of you.

Early evening. One star. Animal longing
as interpreted by the alto sax: cat in heat,
dark heart, incendiary sex. One armchair,
dark green, up-ended, no seat.
One streetlight of pale green light, like the interior
of a grape. One-way street sign, ignored by many.
Two young women, waiting on my front steps:
one with brown eyes, amber almost (fallen angel),
the other with olive green eyes (hungry ghost).

On my street, the lords of the Mayan ball court,
no older than ten, kick a red rubber ball
off the cars and the houses and each other's heads.
In her silver wig the curmudgeon of New Bohemia
wields her broom like a cattle prod. "Animals!
They're everywhere! This town's going to the dogs!
They can't tell a front stoop from a urinal!"
Later on my street, the powerfully-drugged-and-
spirit-vacant will prove her all too true.

I miss having real dogs on my street.
The happy-go-lucky, the devil-may-care,
the eternal nose for possibility. Padding home
softly through the dusk, past the basilica
with its three-tiered bell tower and one gold cross,
past the empty café tables, the ancient barbershop
gone out of business, the new bar billing itself
as a "cure for the blues," little jingle
of dog collar, tail like a metronome.

On my street – overgrown alley, really –
the Spanish have left their mission tiles,

the Victorians their bay windows, brocade drapes,
behind which nosy neighbors scrutinize
all comings and goings. I can't tell who left the iron gates
fronting all these low-rent entranceways. The Ohlone
must have left this four-star sky, slender clouds
somewhere between the color of grilled salmon and neon pink.
Warm air. No wind. The hour of all's well.

It only lasts an hour. Now the chilly insinuations
of fog, and one of my best friends sits in her car
as if she's lost her best friend. Her life has stalled
between two signs that say NO STOPPING. I walk up
and pretend to write her a ticket. "Lady, are you blind?
You're not allowed to be stopping here. Can't you read the sign?
You've got to keep moving. Now if you don't want to
see me in court, I suggest you take me to dinner."
In her laughter a powerful engine is turning over.

Later on my street, the report of gunfire, backfire,
or firecrackers – possibly all of the above. The old ghosts
flee the urine-stink of doorways, the new ghosts settle in
with their lethal apparatus. The dance club pumps out
a narcotic beat, the line is growing longer, faces growing longer.
The curmudgeon has closed for the night her shop of complaints.
The streetlight is now the greenish-yellow eye of a cat,
the fog is the palest pink, what you find inside the petals
of certain hybrids, on the cheeks of nervous virgins,

and the upper flat across the street is lighted
in electric blue: the young Mayan lords are sacrificing
their own lively pure hearts to television…
It's not until later (and later can take years) that you see
these are the rare children who have never known death,
and you see the fallen angel and the hungry ghost are sisters,

and on the curmudgeon's bare arm are blue numbers, tiny but indelible,
and on the front stoops are dime-size drops of dried blood,
and the black dog of my longing is trotting the other way,

and the hour of all's well has passed.

Three years later and I still look for him,
smiling grocer from Beijing, tall as my brother
and who, like him, wore polo shirts and blue jeans,
stylish wire rims, on his wrist a knocked-off Rolex.
A bilingual dictionary lay open like a sacred text, always at the ready
beside a fish bowl stocked with chocolate-dipped biscotti,
and his two girls tripped down the aisles in pinafores
of hyper-color – bubblegum pink, radium green –
while he happily took on "The Battle Hymn of the Republics":
"Mine eyes have seen the gory of the coming of the roared…"
Once, when he confided he worked in China as a doctor –
cardiology, of all things – but that he was stuck
in too much red tape to catch up to who he'd been,
I was embarrassed for him. Though not for long:
his demeanor was an antibiotic for bad luck.
Day-old bread, sold for half-off, he'd give outright
to the nomads next door camped out on cardboard,
and he was so dependably cheerful and guileless,
that time early on when we lost the baby, then each other,
and no one and nothing could be counted on,
I knew enough to pick up a pound of coffee, a can of soup,
as if his store were a rescue mission for all the dispossessed.
The night I told him what I did for a living
he looked impressed in a way that made me believe
he was, and he laughed when I fine-tuned his English,
and I laughed, and it wasn't until later I discovered
the after-dinner mints he had slipped into my bag,
the kind in elegant green foil that hints at hidden treasure.
Times like this, there's a momentary infusion of
– "pleasure" seems too weak a word – but whatever it is,
too often it's treated cheaply: you feel thirsty, go to the sink,
guzzle a drink of water, and never give a thought
to where it came from, or how it got here, or where it's going,

and how it won't be around forever, and now
I have forgotten his name, and that pains me.
What's in a name? Sometimes everything. In that other life
you and I would both say *Bread*
and might as well have been saying *Life*
(though I know we can't always say what we should),
and you would hold up a loaf of sourdough, and I'd ask *Fresh?*
And our heart-doctor-turned-grocer would answer:
*Flesh. Make today.* And we'd both say: *Good.*

I'm nobody until I leave my house.
Then a man for whom the street
is the house he is bound to
tips his old trucker's hat in passing
and wishes me a "Happy New Year, Your Honor."
I should return his good cheer
with some fast food-cum-booze money,
though he hasn't asked for any,
though the spare change that has trickled down
into my pocket is too spare
to trickle into his. At the bank
the teller with the eternal pout
smiles warmly, calls me "Sir," says
what a pleasure it is to see me again.
Suddenly, I'm a magnate of invisible means.
Still, I cross the street quickly
when I catch the wild eye of a bristle-face,
he of the unbuttoned cuffs, trailing shirttail,
untied shoelace, as though he saw me coming –
his would-be patron, his answered prayer –
and rushed to dress for the occasion.
"Please, Allah, I have a job, I swear –
Addis Ababa Market, between Turk and Eddy –
but they say first I must have shave and shower.
I go to YMCA, *they* say five dollars
for shave and shower" – and already I'm turning
away, wondering what the hell I pay my worthless
bodyguards for – "Please, Allah, you give me
the five dollars and I promise you, next week
you come to Addis Ababa, between Turk and Eddy,
and you will have your money back,"
and by now he has secured my arm,
so I pull out a dollar bill so crisp

I could cut his hairy throat. But he counters
with another tack. "No Allah, *five* dollars,
I *beg* of you, *please*, Allah," and the beggar drops
smoothly to his knees, as eons of tradition demand.
The lunching law students, the sweet-smelling future
wanglers of America, are only mildly interested
in this type of negotiation, but I urge him
to get up, *get up*. I have to shout at him
to take the little I'm offering, which is better
than the nothing I imagine he's used to –
and he does, though perfunctorily, no thank you,
no smile, no more invocations of the deity,
his zeal reserved for an easier mark...

And months later, in a city
that is not Addis Ababa, I am back to not being
a circuit judge or an oil sheikh,
but still hear that nagging
*please, Allah, please, Allah*, rising through me
as through a minaret: the open arches far above
the stone floor, the filthy rich and the dirt poor
prostrate on the same prayer rug, bowing to an ancient
and intricate design, the light with its thin fingers
touching every one of them.

X

One little glitch in the genetic code
and I could be waiting forever
in a secondhand coat for a shuttle bus,
my lips moving over the invisible
newsprint my cortex couldn't help
but fabricate. One little hitch
in the helical flow
and I could be standing like cattle
on a cold morning, before the slaughter
that comes, not in one clinical blow,
but little by little, day by day,
a largely quiet beast –
what used to be called "dumb" –
with eyes that look right through you.
The slightest tear in one
sleek chromosome, and I could be trudging
through the week with meaty limbs
and frightwig hair, like our early progenitors,
whose profoundest joys, whatever they were,
were dust by age thirty.
One cruel twist of nucleic acid
and my unkissed face could be swiveling
up the street and down, the object
not of admiration but pity, a child's
lunch pail in one hand, my eyes wide,
my clothes too bright or too big,
inadvertent clown. One glitch,
one hitch, one tear or twist,
and my thick skin could be flayed alive
twice a day – first by the keen laughter
of schoolkids and bums, then by the pointed
indifference of everyone else –

while I wait and wait
for my rescue ride,
and no one comes.

THE ORDERS

One spring night, at the end of my street
God was lying in wait.

A friend and I were sitting in his new sedan
like a couple of cops on surveillance,
shooting the breeze to pass the time,
chatting up the daydreams, the raw deals,
all the woulda-coulda-shoulda's,
the latest "Can you believe that?"
As well as the little strokes of luck,
the so-called triumphs, small and unforeseen,
that kept us from cashing it all in.

And God, who's famous for working
in mysterious ways and capable of anything,
took the form of a woman and a man,
each dressed in dark clothes and desperate enough
to walk up to the car and open the doors.

And God put a gun to the head of my friend –
right against the brain stem, where the orders go out
not only to the heart and the lungs
but to consciousness itself – a cold muzzle aimed
at where the oldest urges still have their day:
the one that says eat whatever's at hand,
the one that wants only to fuck,
the one that will kill if it has to…

And God said not to look at him
or he'd blow us straight to kingdom come,
and God told us to keep our hands
to ourselves, as if she weren't that kind of girl.

Suddenly time was nothing,
our lives were cheap, the light in the car
cold, light from a hospital,
light from a morgue. And the moments
that followed – if that's what they were –
arrived with a nearly unbearable weight,
until we had acquired
a center of gravity
as great as the planet itself.

My friend could hardly speak –
he was too busy trying not to die –
which made me chatter all the more,
as if words, even the most ordinary ones,
had the power to return us to our lives.

And behind my ad-libbed incantation,
my counterspell to fear, the orders
still went out: keep beating, keep breathing,
you are not permitted to disappear,

even as one half of God kept bitching
to the other half that we didn't have
hardly no money at all, and the other half barked,
"I'm telling you to shut your mouth!"
and went on rummaging through the back seat.
And no one at all looking out their window,
no one coming home or going out…

Until two tall neighbors came walking toward us
like unsuspecting saviors… And God grabbed
the little we'd been given, the little we still had,
and hustled on to the next dark street.

MOUNTAIN TOWN

Sometimes hell looks beautiful:
roses pink in May and snow still on the peaks
where, the natives say, a great spirit looks kindly down.
This week, Cinco de Mayo, and half the locals
will get shit-faced on other spirits –
Dos Equis, Corona, Coors – while the rest of town
will hardly stand it, staying home with their Bibles
or elk-skin drums, or the ritual wars
of athletes beamed down by a satellite
that keeps pace with the restless planet.
And at the junior high dance, an American Greek
will leave his ball cap at home, revealing
the streak of white that shoots like rapids
prematurely through his handsome hair. Tonight
he'll find what it takes to approach the Mestiza
whose long black hair is sweeter-looking than licorice.
He'll ask her to dance in that polite voice of his,
and she'll say she can't, her finger hurts.
The rest of his life when a woman says no
he will bring her fingers lightly to his lips.
But now he doesn't give a second glance
to the tall girl with short hair, who hardly ever
says a word in class, but lately has taken to wearing
harem pants, and blouses that bare her slender waist.
He doesn't notice her new glasses, the good job
they do of framing her face, of bringing out the blue
in her shadowed eyes. A girl with a name
like Carey, or Cara, a name in which affection
is present but buried. Last year at school
she broke down at the counselor's. Her father
again. How he took her on a fishing trip
far from town. How he put his hand
where it didn't belong, and whispered her name

for a little kiss, but tried to take much more.
First the all-week binge after his layoff
and slamming her into the wall. And then this.
She has ended up on the immaculate, polished floor
of a foster home, turning in her fingers
his Easter gift, an egg with the same vivid colors
of the room she can never go back to,
a cheerful bright shell that's empty inside.
And what about father, what about him?
With his middle-aged face like dough
bad luck has punched down, his weak eyes magnified
behind their lenses, his sport shirt strictly small town
thrift shop? It's been over a week since his wife
washed her no-color hair, a young woman
not young enough to be missing a tooth where she shouldn't.
A woman whose swollen stomach has nothing to do
with another child: she's drinking now as much as he is;
there are ways of leaving without having to go anywhere.
What was he thinking out there on the lake,
in that hour when you can believe the world
is a place you never want to leave?
I see him casting a line with the flick of a wrist
that wasn't taught any other kind of grace.
I see how undisturbed the water is
when his feathered lure hits. And the dark circle
which repeats itself in ever-widening arcs –
I can see that too, but not where it begins
or where it will end.

## ODE

You want them to write
an ode, a love song
to whatever delights
or defines them, and all they want
is to mock the drone
of the math teacher stuck in the fifties,
whose pants are too short and socks
are white. Or they want
to rattle off the slang
for their greatest curse,
their favorite sport:
the body parts that possess them
and which they yearn to possess,
the latest secret code of sex
they figure you can't decipher.
Or they want, simply,
to be left alone. Look
at this one, huddled inside
his arctic hood, asleep and slumped
toward the open window, explorer
of the other way. Or this one,
who recoils from being made
to speak the little she loves
for fear it will vanish, as so much
already has by her sixteenth year.
You too are afraid: that you don't have
what it takes to touch them
the way they need to be touched,
which is why you want them
to do for themselves, praise
whatever sustains them, whatever
is good and doesn't go away.
And so, how can you not love them

when they answer with anti-odes:
to homework and take-homes,
to slow death by boredom, to the unspeakable
acts their bodies have endured for years
and for which they are only beginning
to find the pathetic and necessary words?
And on your last day, how can you
not love it when the quietest one
is changing at his locker
in a crowded hallway, teasing
the girls as he drops his pants,
the girls pretending they're in shock,
how can you hear him sing,
almost to himself, *I'm the one*
*you love to hate* – young boy smile
on a young man face, the old joy
of self-love still intact – how can you
hear him sing and not want to sing along,
not want to smile back?

## DOJO

If I'm stopped by the laughable
gaggle of little girls at the dojo,
wrapped in their white uniforms
of self-defense and working on their abs,
their ankles held down while they will
their tiny chins to their tiny knees – then

what gets me going again
is the lamentable
high school where I taught
a shy fifteen-year-old
the uses of metaphor, the magic
of calling one thing
by another's name,
and she taught me
in her small voice
to say the everyday straight out,
without reluctance or shame –
in her poem, "baby"
didn't mean "boyfriend"
or "sweetheart," it meant
baby, her baby –

a high school where mine
was the only light face
in a too full room of dark faces,
though I had my own darkness
and kept it to myself,
though they had their own light
and spent it freely, their hands
shooting high at every question,
bodies almost airborne, loud
entreaties for me to call on them,

to let them show off
how much they knew,
how worthy they were
of a hundred attentive ears –

a school that displays on the outside
a visionary's name
and on the inside: a metal detector,
heavy chains on the exit doors
(on the bars called "panic handles"),
and armed guards in uniforms
who have little use
for the clever turn of phrase,
the slangy wit, the heartfelt
sentiment – any lively song
that can make them forget
the world is a deadly place.

What was I doing back in school, site of my early sorrows?
Dreaming as a kind of retrieval system, taking you back to learn
what you left behind, and now need to carry forward.
Back to that classroom, then, where I had little interest
in obeying the dictates of Sister Mary Something or Other
but alas, had no choice. By ten I'd acquired a reputation:
intelligent hellion who, if not careful, would take
that fateful turn down the road of the irredeemable.
At ten I didn't need to hear, again, the doctrinaire
melodrama of redemption, how we were born in sin,
with that big strike already against us,
and how we would end that way – unless we earned
the right to be saved. *To be worthy* is the phrase
that comes to mind, what we prayed for on our knees,
careful not to slip back into the murderous
hatpins the vigilant nuns trained on our behinds.
The savior we beseeched was easy to believe in
because, like us, he came out of a womb, was smarter
than his elders, and cried out his anguish
when those he loved turned away from him,
or seemed to turn. Even at ten we knew the pain
of sudden betrayal, forsaken on the playground,
in the crowded lunchroom, at our own kitchen table.
What we didn't know was the plan, the divine one
in which our suffering was a first-class ticket
to the state of grace. We were too close to misery –
the withering putdown by a teacher, our asses kicked
by grinning assholes after class. And there were those other bruises
brought to school, some visible, some not, shrugged off
with the most suspect excuses. The inequitable
was our sixth sense, and told us we were mad to believe
anything good could come out of something so bad.
We weren't old enough to see the beauty in sacrifice,

in giving up our selfish needs for the greater good.
No one was old enough then, and almost no one would ever be.

But last night, in that dream school, so like the one
where I came of age, I was about to do all of us proud.
I know pride is one of the deadliest sins
but this is the kind where you've been beaten down
by the misguided, the sick, the narrow-minded,
and you'll be damned if you let it go on
another minute. I stood at the blackboard,
yellow chalk in hand, and drew the symmetrical diagram
that would chart my genius for ages to come.
I, who'd always been the archnemesis of numbers,
watched the $x$ coordinate and the $y$
do my bidding, and do it gladly, happy for the chance
to represent at last, not the unknown, but
an intrinsic truth, purest essence made visible.
I don't remember exactly, but it had something to do
with desire. The plotting of desire toward a destiny
unquestionably, and marvelously, inevitable.
One soul, $x$, inviolate from the start, crossed the vacant
spaces before it with only one end in mind:
to encounter $y$, its kindred spirit, its worthy counterpart,
and to be worth itself of such a relation.
It felt so clear, so elegantly obvious, I was ready
to take a shot at the unified field theory –
when Sister Mary Skeptical dispatched me to my seat.
The grid I left behind – the plotting of desire
toward its ideal fulfillment – was clean, precise, brilliant
in its simplicity… And, in the long run, nothing more
than the promise of a promise, the schema of a dream.
Was it so different from the long blocks, the empty squares,
a lover of cities had laid out long before I was conceived,
an architect of intersections, of commerce and cohabitation –
as well as the sudden, maddening, cul-de-sac? The final day

before summer break, my fifth grade teacher, my long suffering exemplar of lovelessness, was in a generous mood. "This child," she said, and she pointed to me, "this child will go a long way." But she never did say where, exactly, that long way led.

What do you know at nineteen, just another of Eros's
undistinguished apprentices, a rank beginner at learning
how quickly beauty can turn to terror
and back again? When you're nineteen the slightest
disturbance must be glad to see you, you're so ready
to be stunned, then shaken, then grateful you're still alive.
Even afterwards, how little you realize what you want to call wisdom
has opened you, not like a window or a door, but a wound.

So at nineteen I pushed through winter drifts,
student of the amorous, dual major in design and desire,
on my way to visit a friend in his life study class.
The nude model that day was our age, at rest
on her side like a Matisse engrossed in TV,
her glossed hair a cascade over one shoulder, leaving
in plain view a perfect breast. Hair I wanted
to call titian, not quite auburn, not quite rust, a color
I'd never seen, would never forget, and would never
be able to name. The same color between her legs,
though I made sure my eyes didn't linger there,
and spread along the whole lissome length of her
was a galaxy of freckles, the lovely dispersion
of constellations, every star a shade of gold.

But what distinguished her beauty from every other
was how naturally she seemed to lie in the sphere
of so much scrutiny, all that surpassing delight
stretched on the circular bed of each trained eye
as if we were there to pay homage, or as if we weren't there
at all. I thought of a word from *Tender Is the Night*
which Fitzgerald had used to damn his protagonist:
*repose.* With every quick glance I took an inventory
of the immanent – the upturned breast, the freckled nose,

the hair, the hips, the hint of derrière – the long
fleshy sine wave of the numinous – and knew she possessed
exactly what I lacked. Doomed as a character
in a tragic romance, I lacked the secret of repose.

My painter friend by this time was a blather
of form and function – this color, blah blah, that line –
when all I knew was that I had to get the hell out of there.
The gods were not kind. The only exit led directly
in front of her. The plan was to sneak out
without a glance – partly out of propriety,
partly out of a sudden sense of shame –
but I looked anyway. It was as if I had been caught
in an unsuspecting trance: she was staring
not at me but *into* me, a look so direct its aim
was to strip me of all defenses, so that *I* became
in that moment the naked one. In Anthro class
I'd heard of a *brujo* – his evil eye could make you feel
you were being disemboweled on the spot.
Your powers of mind, your vaunted will – useless
against the mystery. Now this bold stare would take its place
in my education as a lover, this latest cut
of the old saw, *If looks could kill…*

It took many years before I passed
from apprentice to journeyman, a spiraling
by turns ascendant and descendant, many more wounds
that went unexplained before I came to know
just how true it is that a mere look can do us in.
We move through a world that's treacherous
with expectation, and we're enthralled by the virtual –
what *could* be, after all, is so much more enticing
than what *is* – and then comes the vacant and unreachable
face of someone you knew from the outset
you shouldn't grow closer to, but did.

Or the hapless friend you try in your way to help
and can't, who without warning snaps at you
with teeth bared and a feral glint in the eyes.
Or the stranger late at night, a coat draped over one arm,
the fabric rich and finely spun, who walks up to you
calm and smiling, as if to ask for the time –
the stranger as a wealth of possibilities –
and who says, *I have a gun, I'll shoot you.*
*Give me everything you have. Don't look at me.*

# NOTE

A note from my special agent in the field:
she has seen the mystery bird of May
I myself have never seen. A year ago
I'd hear these liquid notes –
three short, one long – not every day,
maybe twice a week, but for months, clear
into fall, and not once
could I catch sight
of the mystery singer. A silvery
riff near the rooftops, little lord
of the power lines, a song
that one day came out of nowhere
and belonged to the open air.
And, one day, was gone.

Now, a year later – one more
turning around our master star,
each year turning faster
than the one before – she says
this morning, on her walk to work,
she heard those four notes
that seemed to declare
a gentle warning, a kind of
wake-up call. She says the tree
was thin, without leaves,
and the bird, not surprisingly,
plain and small. Of course, I think,
it would have to be.
Tricky beauty. Comes back
to arouse when it wants to.
Gives the dead air
lessons in inspiration.
Gives the intensest

pleasure (itself a brief song
that will play
long after it's gone).
But never, or almost never,
gives itself away.

The night we met we went for a drive
and parked by some trees near the village square
and compared all the deaths we knew up till then.
The ones where the body took its leave
and the spirit, still alive, stayed close at hand.
The ones where the spirit was a mere ghost of itself
and the abandoned body, lingering, would languish.
And the most difficult death to say out loud,
where body and spirit had gone so far
nothing – not wish or prayer or will –
would ever bring them back.

And when we were done we sat in the car,
in the deserted square, and said nothing.
Whisper of fountain water. The streetlamps
old-fashioned, round as the moon and as empty.
When the moon is between constellations,
between those lucent bodies some look to
for direction, it's said to be void-of-course,
and that is what we were, caught in a solitary drifting,
and glad, I think, for the quiet and the company.

I don't know if what happened next
you'd want to call remarkable, but
she tilted her head back on the seat
in what seemed like supplication, a longing
for the kind of respite I didn't know
if I could provide. The nearest human being
was no closer to us than the nearest star,
and I remember looking down at her hand,
which was faint as a star, and thinking: touch it.
When it comes to healing, hands are good –
they know the most about receiving, and holding close,

and of course letting go. But the face is also good –
the face, some say, is everything –
accustomed as it is to keeping everything
time has given it. She turned her face

toward mine, and I leaned my face towards hers,
and when I slid back the hair that hid her cheek
it smelled like the earth – like something we had loved
a few light years ago, when body and spirit were one –
and an old calm filled the close air between us,

aromatic as an herb, deep as a kiss... So that now
when I break a sprig of rosemary under my nose
and remember what it is to live on the earth,
remember the many endings, the dull hard drift
of helplessness, I also remember this.

To enter you bend low as a beggar
calling on the last resort.
Clutch your little stalk of sage,
take your place in the circle, the entrance flap
closing behind you, the darkness closing in.
When the voice of the man called Grandfather
asks who has come for healing,
you raise your hand like a schoolchild
when it's your voice, clear and sure,
he wants to hear. *Who has come for healing?*
And you don't know what it is in you
that asks as much for others as for yourself,
that wants what enduring good there is
to find in you its resourcefulness.
What else in your life has proved you worthy
of such a burden? The heat when it comes
is so dense, the darkness so impenetrable,
the air so scarce, it feels like dying.
Now you understand those ancient illustrations
where the soul is leaving the body through the mouth –
or is it an evil spirit, a demon out-demoned?
So dark, so hard to breathe, it feels like living:
all you ever have is your body and your breath
and the desire to get from one moment to the next
without succumbing. When someone suddenly
cries out for help, you can easily believe
only the resourceful will survive, can take on faith
that what heals and is healed is the same –
you'd be dead by now if you didn't believe it,
one of the weeping ghosts at Grandfather's feet.
The cry goes out again, terrified, terrifying,
a voice you've been close to, it seems, for years,
a questioning cry it's not your place to answer.

To do nothing now but wait is the burden before you.
And to keep your place in this circle of vital purpose,
a circle that needs you present to stay complete.
Whatever the matter is, you're to remain here
long enough to know the heart of it,
the demon-pain you haven't learned to assuage.
If you need help – and you will need help –
ask. But remember: when help comes
it doesn't say, Oh you poor thing – here,
let me make it all better. Help says,
Lie down. Pray hard. Use your sage.

I thought summer was over.
The black cherries of August,
voluptuous in their bowl of pale green –
nowhere to be seen in early October.
I thought it was all gone, the long days,
the heat, pilgrimages to the park, the beach,
the warm nights worshiped for their indolence,
the dark doorways lined with Spanish tiles
where years ago after so many margaritas
we took refuge from a sudden deluge,
rain, kiss, rain, kiss, rain. I thought,
in my hopelessly practical, know-it-all way,
sweet summer was over. No more gypsy guitar chords
for the aficionados of twilight. No more
forbidden passwords, whispered in the ear,
that would admit us to the dangerous
and the thrilling. The old year was lying down
to die. Soon the streets would teem with ghosts,
hand-in-hand with ghouls. Soon the cranial
pleasures, the candy skulls and cookie skulls,
the gaudy sugars of death that feed the need
to remember, the need to sweeten memory.

And then, at one of those intersections
where the unexpected is always waiting,
like stands of tropical fruit even in winter,
bright presences in the grim pit of the year,
I met her again. Those eyes, large and dark, as solemn
as they were sensual. Her formidable necklace
of teeth, jaguar or shark. And her hair, that long pouring
of dark wine I could never drink enough of.
Beauty that evoked from total strangers
something close to lamentation, prayerful moans,

a kind of reverential agony. *Te soñé*, she said,
*I dreamt you.* Groceries in her arms, the girl
and the boy she had always wanted
hugging her loose skirt of pink dahlias
whose petals would never fall. *Te soñé*, she smiled,
*I'll tell you later*, and when she turned to go
her hair, dark as black cherries in August, her hair
was a dream that would never stop coming true.
A dream that did precisely what she meant it to:
it stopped the sullen, distracted year, called it
back, as if it had been foolish enough to forget
something absolutely essential, something
that should have never been left behind.

The crackpot on the train to the racetrack
made it sound so easy. "We're gonna make a lot
of money, and not the old-fashioned way, either.
We won't have to *earn* it. We're gonna *win* it."
Nose runny, laughter a wheeze, he didn't seem to faze
the corporate commuters deep in their routines,
the morning edition scanned three columns at a time,
suit jackets folded just so before a snooze.
A slinky blonde in black appeared to be doing an impression
of a slinky blonde in black – not bad, but needed work –
while on the upper deck in back, a young man, dark,
was plinking the tines of a kalimba.
Crackpot said, "Say I bet the 9 horse at 10 to 1
and 9 comes in. I go to the window
and they give me a bunch of money" –
as if this were a school bus and all of us
children or idiots, lacking the merest notion
of what it means to gamble, much less to win…

Actually, I've been on that bus:
a hulk of pale orange the school district junked
and my father and his cronies resurrected,
painting it celestial blue, a godsend to deliver them
from Utica to the pearly starting gates of Vernon Downs.
What's it like, a frolic to the racetrack down Seneca Turnpike
through the green of irrepressible hope? Corny songs
on the PA, cigar smoke issuing from the driver's window,
wives shifting smoothly through the gears of gossip.
Several of the men – a couple of whom, like Padre, were amateur
middleweights with short careers – will go a few rounds
of verbal sparring. Unspoken Rule #1: Nobody fights dirty.
Unspoken Rule #2: Do it in fun. They have named themselves
The Idiots' Club. It was on this bus that Padre

first explained the big money bets –
Daily Double, Exacta, Perfecta – prospects
however meager that were enough to distract us
from what Padre once called "this pathetic life."
Aunt Rose had been performing the miracle called
"chicken cacciatore" and saying the rich
had problems too, money guaranteed nothing (a story
only a saint could make stick). Then Padre's complaint:
"Well it's too bad *we're* not rolling in it,
then we wouldn't have to put up with this
pathetic life…" The silken darkness

of haunches, the vivid motley of jockey silks –
it was my father who introduced me
to longshots and lucky hunches, to the heart-thudding
grandstand turn, the come-from-behind surge
down the homestretch, right down to the wire –
down to the lightning flash of a photo finish –
and then the proud trot to the winner's circle.
He was the one I'd pore over the forms with, glasses
midway down our noses, like physician and intern
on a consultation: thumbing the exotic names, the elegant bloodlines,
marking the strengths, who'd been tested, how well they'd done,
then a likely prognosis. And he was the one
I'd commiserate with over the also-rans,
the losers by a neck or a nose, or – true disgust –
by twenty lengths: some long-necked beauty, nervous or spooked,
who'd broken stride on the back stretch
long before turning home… When one of us won
we were winners together. Coolly, without pride,
he'd peel off a couple of bills
to front my new ventures, or with fellow Idiots
take encouragement from my latest triumph,
smacking his lips, bug-eyed over the next lineup.
Then, with a cartoon grin, he'd drop his dentures.

The loony tune on the train, though, had all of us beat,
the kind of hairy-eared oddball my father's a master at impersonating.
Someone mentioned Folsom Street and the guy said, "Folsom?
That ain't a street, that's a prison! Yeah, I swear
I just escaped from there" – sly grin, licking his chops,
tickled by his own performance. I was tickled too
thinking what Padre would do with this song-and-dance.
We were rolling along, a hazy day, absurdly warm
for November, the blurred city out of sight, out of mind,
the industrial parks gliding past – all so easy –
when, abruptly, our car and the one in front of us
uncoupled, a detachment no one noticed right away.
Crackpot's sermon on Pick Six as "the true salvation"
had the young blonde nodding off behind her shades,
while the kalimba player put me in mind of a place
too charming to exist except in the mind –
and then, long before our anticipated stop,
we began, eerily, to lose momentum…

And looked up to find at the end of the aisle
a door of white space, as if this were truly
the end of the line. Everything went quiet then,
every trial and tribulation, all our inexplicable ways
of being in the world. Odds were even
we'd be late for post time, but disappointment
was slow in coming. We'd been released
into the unexpected – by turns disconcerting, comical,
and strangely calming. So when the train sped on
without us, and the sun struck its glass head-on,
a light too harsh to look at long,
we raised our hands to our eyes – as if we were at the beach
or blessing ourselves in church – raised our hands
on what seemed for a moment the threshold
of some kind of heaven.

## TREMOR

In the middle of my life the earth moves hard
against itself, enough to tremble the bed

but not wake me all the way
out of my sleep, and I don't know why

but another tremor goes through me then,
the name of someone I loved in my less than perfect way

who's been gone now who knows how long,
whose passing didn't even twitch the needle

on the scale of the world – and then the tremor
of another name, and I'm waking up

more by the moment, this one gone, that one gone –
father, mother, uncle, aunt – and now lover,

close friend, teacher, idol, leader,
lover again – not only mine but everyone's. Gone,

just like that – a shock that begins with fear
and would end in grief,

if not for the aftershock
of *I'm still here, you're still here.*

Three weeks of rain. Four weeks. Five.
They say we come from the sea.
Carry certain depths wherever we go.
What light is available doesn't reach us.

Seven weeks of rain. Eight weeks. Nine.
Life this deep is dark and slow.
You hardly know now who you are.

Then, week ten, the kind of twilight
so warm and clear you're almost inclined
not to trust it. The kind of weather
that keeps you walking and walking
because walking is a pleasure again.

*Late night late night –*
the street corner hustler's song
to sell you a transfer on the local line.
I've always wondered: Does the demand
ever meet the supply? And who is it
supplies the supply?

Moon in its baby fingernail phase,
the dark side still discernible.

Keep walking, don't break stride
when someone says to someone: "You goddamn
piss me off – *and you keep on doing it.*"
Reminds me of who used to say: "I look forward
to knowing you the rest of my life."
Well, fare forward, ultimate stranger,
and fare well. *Late night late night –*

And who was it just said:
"I think about calling you every day"
but doesn't call at all? Who was it?
I mean beyond the face, beyond the voice and the name.

A dirigible, cold white, drifts over the skyline,
turns slowly toward the neighborhood, like a shark
that has picked up the scent of blood
but is taking its time, warning signal
on, off, on, off...

And who is it does call me every day?
I mean beyond the voice, beyond the name and the face.

Pastel sweaters on a chainlink fence,
old jackets for sale, shoes abandoned
for a better life: ghost clothes
waiting for the body that will save them
from their suspended animation.

Then blocks later, the same clothes
on a different fence. And look:
the same moon, the same blimp,
the same incantation
aimed at the same passersby
*Late night late night*
*Late motherfuckin' night* – In a parked car
someone says to someone: "Oh and I suppose
*you're* so virtuous." The night is
duplicating itself, as if it means to last.

I reach for the bus pass tucked
in the deep pocket of my old jacket –
and find instead the sea stone,
small, smooth, dark – the night's

hidden, enduring heart –
the sea stone that someone (who was it?)
gave me years ago, for good luck.

III.

Mindfulness must be engaged.

    *– Thich Nhat Hanh*

> Seeing the world driven by passion, seeing
> it steeped in sorrow, the bodhisattva
> dedicates himself to the enlightenment of
> all mortals. He is characterized by
> compassion spontaneously present but
> devoid of preconception...

I'm called and I go, not quite a bodhisattva,
not knowing what to expect, to greet as I would a friend
victims of stroke, failing hearts, childhood polio.
I sit over tea, a meager sandwich, a bruised
piece of fruit, while they apologize for not having
more to offer. Or I sit by their beds, though
I'm no doctor, and listen to their breath cut short
by the wounds time has not diminished,
and I see behind their eyes the certain death
they are fleeing again, hopeful if destitute.

And what I can't let them know
is how poor I feel to offer them nothing but my ear.
How I am made to suffer in silence their own
fierce suffering. This one, seventy-nine, aphasic,
living alone: "I left Bremen in '38, came here
to this country when I was twenty-seven..."
Her blue eyes go gray, her voice barely survives
the abrupt trip back to the Holocaust. A dark spot
on my golden delicious, I cut it out. "Oh you must come
to real dinner," she moans, wiping her eyes,

and doesn't catch me wiping my own.
"What are these flowers?" I ask. In a vase
of clear glass, their petals are huge, dusky pink as
the rouge on her face, dead at the edges. "Those

are my roses, I grow them myself!" She dives deep
for their name, past the fear of forgetfulness,
past shame, and comes up sputtering. "C-C-Countess…"
Even in decline they cry out for someone
to sing their praises. She tries out my name.
"Centaur-Centaur-ella…" On her stunned tongue

I've become half-man, half-horse, in her quiet house
I've entered the mythic. The trees of the park across the street
are timeless trees, not fin-de-siècle sycamore
or the ghostly beeches of Buchenwald. The exquisite figurines
on her coffee table – a silver fox, a boy with a ball –
have escaped the dark woods of history. Beside the typewriter,
a suitcase that refuses to close, stuffed with a lifetime
of stories, could be anyone's life, could be all of our stories
put together… At the door she's a grande dame, takes my cold hand
in her warm ones. "Oh you are so wonderful, Mr. Gentleman of the
    Century."

From centaur to gentleman: so, I've become human again.

A few hours spent in the dry rooms of the dying.
Then the walk home, and the sudden rain
comes hard, and you want it coming hard,
you want it hitting you in the forehead
like anointment, blessing all the days
that otherwise would be dismissed
as business as usual. Now you're ready
to lean on the rail above the empty diamonds
where, in summer, the ballplayers wait patiently
for one true moment more alive than all the rest.
Now you're ready for the ancient religion of dogs,
that unleashed romp through wildness, responding
to no one's liturgy but the field's and the rain's.
You've come this far, but you need to live further in.
You need to slip into the blind man a while,
tap along with his cane past the market stalls
and take in, as if they were abandoned,
the little blue crabs which in an hour will be eaten.
You have to become large enough to accommodate
all the small lives that otherwise would be forgotten.
You have to raise yourself to the power of ten.
Love more, require less, love without regard
for form. You have to live further in.

## SISTER

Slow dark woman in a straw hat
turns down my street with her face in her hands,
crying, not loud, but enough to be heard.
Slow dark woman darker than me
though each hand boasts the rings of royalty.
Woman I want to call Sister, the way they do
in the faraway state she started from.

Sister (I think), I like your little gold crosses,
how they bring to your dark ears
the last glint of daylight.
But tell me, Sister, where
is your king of kings,
where is your savior now?

*

I pass her on the way to my house
and don't look back. These days
the desperate will try anything
to get what they need. How many I've trusted
conned me out of more than I care to admit.

But I look anyway. Can I afford
to ask if she's all right?

Can I afford not to?

*

"Are you OK?" And she walks by,
her hands locked over her face

like the gates of a prison
or a city under siege.

"What's wrong?" These days
the simplest question can be
the surest way of asking for trouble.

And trouble is what I get,
the whole story of trouble.

It begins with the sound of grief,
a burbling like a broken toilet,
none of it intelligible.
I wait it out. I must spend
half my life waiting
for everyone's words to make sense.

And then, as if transmitted
over a weak wavelength:
*daughter... fourteen... pregnant...*
*my son, he eighteen, a new father...*

And her husband in county jail
for beating her just short of murder.
She's waiting to see if the judge
will hit him back with a –
"What you call it?"
"A restraining order."

Other than all that, she's glad
for the rehab downtown
that keeps her off crack.
But it worries her she's not working.
The government check wouldn't feed a cat,

the street's too close and the bottle
never too far away, and husband's
due back in less than a week.
Chocolate face, black cherry mouth,
she looks good enough to eat.
It's tough, I tell her –
what else am I going to say?
I know I can't help her back
to what she really wants.
"It all come down," Sister says,
"all at once."

*

My own sister, in her mid-twenties and unmarried,
in love only with the glass pipe of fantasy, gave up
her cinnamon-skinned infant to a foster home.
And, on the very day she was due to begin
her own coming to terms with her cocaine *daimon,*
left all of us behind for parts unknown.

When I asked my father where he thought she'd gone,
his face tensed in the way of those too intimate
with disappointment. This man who taught me by example
everything I needed to know – that what matters
is the alleviation of pain – when I asked this man
where my sister was, and his face tensed, and he whispered
*The dens…* what could I have given him
to alleviate *his* pain?

What wouldn't I have given him?

*

Slow desolate woman
and I, unwitting witness to desolation,
we start talking babies. Life
demands this much of us.
Her new granddaughter's Jameela;
my new niece, Mariah.
Funny how we name these others
before we'll name ourselves.
She's smiling now and I tell her
how nice her smile is. I tell her
my name, and she says "Linda."
That's Spanish for "pretty," I say.
She takes my hand and is slow
to let go: now that the glint is gone
from her little gold crosses,
she will haul her cares back
through "Valencia Gardens" –
windows barred, windows boarded up,
and the latest local craze:
bloated bags of garbage disemboweled on the street.
Back to the stenciled gray walls that decree
"No Trespassing by Non-Tenants,"
and the men with too much time on their hands
in T-shirts that howl SHUT UP BITCH.
She swears she'll get out before it does her in.
"Project ain't no way for a person to live."

What a word, *project.*
Every day's a goddamned project.

          *


She wants to know if she can call me sometime.
"I'll be around," I say. "Keep that smile going,"
though I know better, and so does she.

But walking away, she beams me her best.
"I know God sent you to me," she says.
"God sent you to me in my darkest hour..."

Oh Linda, oh Sister, darker than me
and lovelier in your desolation,
you don't know, do you,
how much we need each other.

# DER ROSENMEISTER

1.

A woman's voice waking me Sunday morning,
floating in from the weedy patch of dirt
that's my landlady's sorry excuse for a garden.
A high-pitched voice, but not the insect whine
of the oppressed landowner. A woman, but not the woman
who sleeps beside me, murmuring sometimes
troublesome things I know to be true
and wish were otherwise. A soft contralto
I have never heard, saying, "This is Ellen,
and this is Betty Prior. Now where
is Madame Alfred Carrière?"

2.

I pull on my robe and investigate.
A big sweaty man with a baby face
is on his hands and knees, pulling weeds,
and a smaller man in sunglasses, digging holes
for many pots of thorny stalks.
With his little voice the big man says
he's sorry if he woke me up.
He's putting in roses where my overwrought
landlady planned to pour concrete,
threatened by rodents in this
the seventh year of drought, damned
if she'd let a gang of thirsty rats
overrun her squalid strip of dirt.
"Where is Madame Alfred Carrière?"
again inquires the Master of Roses,
and his helper says, "Over here," and guides
the cutting called Madame to a corner plot

as if to the best table in the restaurant.
"Good good good," says der Rosenmeister,
who then lays out a spread of redwood mulch.
"Now where is Intrigue? And Touch of Class?
And Happy? Where the hell is Happy?"


3.


A young man, big, with a baby face,
who bends slowly to his spade, slowly
to his hand rake and hand hoe.
A little needle patched to his arm
I don't want to look at
too closely. And propped
against the wall: an old man's cane.


4.


Next door, in his own sorry plot
he's done wonders
with hybrids: slender smooth stems
taller than the tallest showgirls, luscious
blooms of lemon-coral-peach
even in gloomy December. The bleak
projects are half a block away,
past the barbed wire of the parking lot
and the iron bars by the front doors
we unlock to join the world.
But over the fence that divides
my province from his, the dragonflies,
the "sewing needles," stitch the air,
diligent workers, tireless,
pulling an endless thread
between an invisible heaven
and a too visible earth.

5.

Nasty aphids cling
to the green buds,
they're gnawing the new
leaves down to nothing…

I must confer at once
with der Rosenmeister.

6.

In the stairwell outside
my iron gate, an insect
of a man is startled
out of his fetal dream.
He hurries to his feet, drops a small vial – *Shit* –
his fingers like frantic feelers,
recovers his insect loot,
and scurries down the street.

7.

But der Rosenmeister is not at home.
He's laid up in the hospital,
his landlord says. Bad case
of the flu or something.
I ask him if he knows anything
about aphids. "Aphids?"
"Yeah, they're all over my roses."
He looks at me as if to say,
You're just too plain stupid for words,
but says, "Get some heavy-duty bug spray
and blast the bejesus out of them."

8.

In this, the seventh year of drought,
my landlady – in spattered jeans and workshirt,
painter's cap backwards on her beleaguered head –
my landlady bitches about dry rot, and peeling paint,
and cracks that forever need caulking.
And there's the damned water allotment
the city has imposed. She gives Madame Alfred C.
the evil eye, as if Nature is perpetrating a crime
against itself. She doesn't mention the crackheads
nodding on my front steps, the latest car window
glittering in a million blue-green pieces by the curb
like a spilled cache of rare gems. And no mention
of the recent rash of beatings by baseball bat,
and not always for money – a new blood sport in the neighborhood –
or the screams of bloody murder at four in the morning
that jerk me out of good dreams to dial 911.

No mention of anything she doesn't own or control.

Instead, she scrapes and sands and spackles and paints,
she fills each crack with a white glop and a black curse,
she even cuts off water designed merely to drip, drip
enough to feed the lovely, lovingly installed
roots of American Beauty, and White Lightnin',
and slow-to-bloom Intrigue.

9.

A little peace and quiet. That's all I want
on Sunday morning. Rattan chair
on a carpet of light, portable breakfast
next to the roses, and the heavy paper

that takes hours to read. No puttering
muttering malcontent, swearing
she's going to sell the place.
Even on Sunday I have to wave away
each airborne attack of aphids
who take my cherry Danish
for a new kind of bloom.
Where's der Rosenmeister
when you need him…

                A high voice
comes floating then from its high porch.
"You should take your hose and
give the roses a good hard shower."
"What about bug spray, wouldn't that
be more effective?" "Personally," he says,
"I've had enough toxins for one day."

10.

Demented landlady, never leaving well enough alone.
When she goes away, I water.
When I go away, I worry.

11.

And when I come back
the blood-red petals
are down. A few stems
have aged to brown
with startling speed.
Even the aphids are gone,
off to settle
on something with a future.

Outside his building
der Rosenmeister is collapsed
like Christ of the *Pietà*
in the arms of a paramedic.

12.

I soak the hard earth
per his instructions,
prune the stalks down
to the first cluster of four leaves.
Then I wait.

I wait a good week
for the new life…

Nothing.

I wait two weeks.
Three…

Still nothing.

13.

Maniacal landlady, on hands and knees,
grunting through the latest grout work
like a sow with her snout an inch from the dirt.
Her cohort from next door has his own complaint.
"Son of a bitch had AIDS
and they wouldn't let me evict him."

14.

In late November, when it's expected
the summer pleasures that intoxicate
should be nothing more than memory,
a lush, heady burst of rose
stares me in the face.

And that night, late,
I come home to a moon
that floats
like a cream-white petal
in a black pool.

15.

Yes, I love Rilke's fig tree,
how all year it holds itself in,
and then without fanfare
bursts with a fleshy abundance
to make up for all the dry spells.
But I also love this garden of roses,
the burgeoning, the avid sprawl
in this, the eighth year of drought.
The petals wet, drunk on their own fragrance,
destined to surrender to the inevitable.
And the bent-over stalks, slender,
tougher than they look, how long
they can go without water,
and then, one day, surprise you with a single bud
more dazzling, in the end, than an entire bouquet.

I love this coming to fruition in fits and starts,
this here today gone tomorrow,
this maybe I looked like

I was gone forever, but I'm back —
if not forever, at least for now.

16.

The Master of Roses
is dead. Long live
the Master of Roses.

# THE WOMAN OF THREE MINDS

1.

She tells me she will find a letter
lying around the house – she lives
on the bay, she's intimate
with gray areas, with ebb and flow –
and she'll recognize the handwriting
as her own, but not what the sentences
mean to say. It's as if a cunning stranger
broke in when she wasn't home
and left these thoughts behind
for her benefit. Except, she says,
I have no idea what they mean.
And I'm afraid to read between the lines.

2.

And there's the local grocery store.
The old guy glued to his little TV
who winks at her when she comes in.
Last week, before she could open her mouth,
he tossed a pack of cigarettes on the counter.
"There you go," he said. It was some kind of joke
she didn't get. "I'm sorry," she said,
"but I don't smoke." "You mean you quit?"
"No, I mean I've never smoked."
The old guy laughed. "That's a good one.
You're always pulling my leg." And she saw
he was serious, this near stranger, laughing
at the antics of another near stranger.

3.

When she walked across the crowded yard
of the maximum-security prison, the only woman
for miles, for years, an anesthetist on her way
to ease the stricken inmates into a useful sleep,
the healthy bold ones out for exercise
would edge close to the line they couldn't cross
without catching a bullet from the guards,
and they would take turns making sure she heard
all the usual four-letter words, plus their favorite
five-letter one, all the vilest fantasies
describing what goes where, and for how long,
and to what end – the manic vengeance of men
without hope, human souls who had begun their lives
exactly as she had.

4.

She told me she could handle any one of them.
Fear not a factor. None of them could come close,
she said, to what my father did to me.
Nonetheless, she couldn't wait to get one of them
on her table. A spinal tap would scare anyone
into humility, but when they found out who
was attending them, they'd freak. And what if
she let on she recognized them from the yard
and wasn't having a particularly good day?
And one day, as it happened, she got her wish:
the hard time ringleader, fresh out of solitary,
a man for whom fear was not a factor either.

5.

His life was in her hands
but he worked his angles anyway. She couldn't know
who he was. He'd scam her with his best
model-inmate charm. Told her he'd known his share
of lookers, but she belonged in the movies,
not a hospital for degenerates. Even as she slipped
the needle in, he remained the smiling gentleman,
he made sure to hang on her every word,
never took his eyes off hers. She let him
play it out a while, it was the most amusement
she'd had in months. Then she interrupted him.
You know, she said, I know who you are.
It would be so easy to make sure
you never opened your mouth again.

6.

I walked down the dark pier once
where she lives alone in a simple house
that floats like a promise of safety
in a world of hidden dangers. All the lights out
except for one – the eerie purple neon
of an aquarium. If you stopped and looked hard,
you could see a night heron like the ghost of a bird
settled on a piling that was like death itself:
you couldn't see it, but you knew it had to be there.
And abandoned by the ramp to her front door:
the pale pink bicycle of a six-year-old.

7.

Do you know that poem, she asked me,
"I was of three minds, / Like a tree /
In which there are three blackbirds"?
It's something like that, except I never know
which mind will take over, or when.
But, I said, it's getting better for you, isn't it?
I guess so, she said… But I could see in her eyes
the small craft of the self slipping from its moorings,
pulled off to wherever the cold current would take it.
Yes, I'm better, she said, but with you I switch a lot:
I have no defense against kindness.

8.

And I have no defense against helplessness,
the bête noire that springs up on a moment's notice:
a child, for instance, made to hide in the upstairs bathroom,
made to cower at the creak of someone mounting the stairs,
someone who had helped to create her world, and now,
night after night, is tearing it apart, limb by slender limb.
A child I can't save from the dreaded *snick snick*
of the door handle, which will turn too many times, even years later
in her own triple-locked house, as she sleeps in a loft bed, face down,
her hands folded over what she calls, for good reason, her privates.

9.

After the hardtimer in the prison hospital
realized she valued respect over revenge,
he put out the word. The next day, as she crossed the yard,
one nightmare after another let her pass
without a sound. And then, at the end of the line,

a man with a scar from brow to jaw
bowed deeply and said, Good morning, ma'am,
and how are we today? And she said, We're just fine, thank you.
I looked at the woman of three minds and thought:
There are three important things in life. The first
is to be kind. The second is to be kind. And the third
is to be kind.

TOUCH

This man in shirtsleeves who speedwalks to the exit
with his head down – he's like a celebrity
who wants to keep his life to himself. *I'm not here,*
he seems to be saying. And I'm not here
to see my doctor, but I'm glad to see him anyway.
I'm glad to see anyone who laughs when it's appropriate,
who answers all my questions, who knows what he's doing
and does it well. When I'm sick and too ill at ease
his presence alone encourages faith in the enterprise.

But today he's in a hurry. No time to stop,
shake hands, ask after my health –
not that I need him to – but I have to admit
his hastiness disturbs me, no time
even to look me in the eye.

Without his white coat he looks like someone
in his own care, someone put upon, shamefully
underpaid or underappreciated –
a bus driver, maybe, or a schoolteacher –
someone who, day after day, takes people
where they need to go. His middle-aged head
hunched over like a tonsured monk's, the bald spot
adds to his brown eyes more tenderness –
though maybe he doesn't know from holiness or tenderness,
he only knows he's got eleven minutes for lunch.

He sips his coffee on the run
and maybe a little voice reminds him:
I'm the one without insurance
and he's the safety net
I still owe a couple of hundred.

Or maybe his trouble started long before work,
the nightmare words he goes to bed with
(and wakes to, sometimes, long before rising):
*Malpractice. Metastatic. Immune deficient.*
"No rest for the weary," says the little voice
inside my head, the exhausted sigh
of my first physician. "No rest for the weary,"
my mother laments. And no one mentions
efficient death – which is not exactly the cure
or long vacation most of us have in mind.

That time I thought I would die –
was so bad off I almost wanted to –
the pain was like a long needle
inserted slowly into my abdomen,
pain that had me doubled over like a voodoo victim,
pain that came in waves, a dreaded repetition
that had me rocking on the edge
of the examining table, had me dressed
in a white sheet and moaning like a ghost...

How amazing, then, my doctor's palpation:
relief – immediate, palpable –
delivered by his simple touch alone.

But today he looks as if he could use a doctor himself.
Who is it gives to the giver
when there's never an empty seat in the waiting room,
and the phones jangle his nerves all week
with emergencies, and imagined afflictions, and too real
turns for the worse? How long can he go on gladly
with the free advice, the blissful prescription,
the cheerful word and timely intervention
that never quite come back to him in kind?

Maybe, today, he himself is sick and tired...

And maybe I don't know the first thing about my doctor
and that's the problem: we don't know enough
about those who tend us in our pain. Who touch us
not for love – though love is there – but for life.

In memoriam:
Doctor Joseph McGovern

The day they told me how bad he'd gotten
I drove out like a country doctor, directions
on the dashboard, glad for good weather.
On the radio, *Fanfare for the Common Man,* Copland's woodwinds
arriving in time for the bridge that connects
great city to great headlands, magnificence to magnificence.
Then up the narrow road, steep and shadowed,
that leads from one deadman's curve to another,
and I pictured him in bed – half here on IV,
half gone to the next world – and thought how
any day I could take that kind of turn,
you could take that kind of turn,
and survive it, maybe. Maybe not.

Three to eight weeks, they told me,
and that's it, he's done. I sat close
and didn't say much. This high up, the great city
a haze, the bay out of sight, the light relentless,
advice seemed thin. I preferred his color, like a man
on vacation, his forearm thick as a tree limb,
his voice a little hoarse but still his.
"The Dilaudid," he said, "isn't as good as heroin
but it's good." (Physician to himself, physician
to the end.) I handed him crushed ice in a paper cup
and settled back. It was clear: we two
were on a course for the one elusive truth
beyond the obvious facts.

Time passed. Faint voices outside his room
faded, disappeared. The trees beyond his deck

looked overexposed. I said: What do you see ahead
for yourself? And his prognosis was closer
to that of a seer: "I'm coming back. As a spirit."
His itinerary: check on Marilyn and their garden roses,
on his distant son in Philadelphia (for spirits,
just a jaunt), and on his favorite writing class
(he hated being a dropout at sixty-five; for Dr. Joe
death was a mere hiatus, an inconvenient one).
I asked for some slack before he paid me a visit,
and he perked up at the thought of catching me
in flagrante delicto, and our laughter held nothing back.

A good note for me to leave on. But not for him.
One of us was overcome by the idea of leaving
and he would show me how it was done.
So back we went, years, to the first time he died:
the sudden embolism, heart rate flat, his floating
clear out of his bones, up to the ER's ceiling, where
as a spirit above the grim proceedings, he thought:
Is this all it is? This isn't so bad... I suppose
when I squeezed his arm goodbye and said I loved him,
I was trying to invoke the one word that would sound
a daunting hex on loss. But after all
Dr. Joe was the doctor. "Yeah," he croaked,
"it's always harder on those who have to hang around.
Believe me, I know."

LUCK

Intoxicating weather, like a drug from the East.
The moon full and Levantine, early lights on the hills,
the locals floating to dinner on the magic carpet of the sidewalk.
Weather so warm you can get away with wearing
next to nothing. Heat that even strips the brain,
so that come evening all you want to do
is think of what to eat and drink.

Which was always fine with Sito, my mother's mother,
who seemed to live for the care and feeding of visitors.
Sito of the green eyes, of the earlobes as long as Buddha's,
of the water pipe inlaid with tiny mirrors
the shape of diamonds. She knew the way
to cool hot tempers down: simply set the table.
Ice in a glass, the gold effervescence of ginger ale,
that sharp fizz shooting up your nose. And then
her *lavash*, her flat bread, unleavened and fresh,
thin as a love letter from another country.
And *leban*: yogurt soup, chilled, with sliced cucumber
and mint leaves plucked from the side of her house.
Then the pièce de résistance: a tin sheet
of *kibbeh*, ground lamb mixed with pine nuts
and cracked wheat, scored into diamond shapes
and baked into a crisp lusciousness.
If Sito lived to feed us, then in her house
we lived to be fed. Not for nothing
did a lucky horseshoe hang above her kitchen door.

And now this evening, so slow to relinquish the day's warmth,
I sit at a corner table in La Méditerranée,
the candle jar inlaid with tiny mirrors the shape of diamonds,
the candlelight making jewels of the green eyes
of the woman across from me. Someone who's never tasted

the creamy tartness of *leban*, who opens her mouth
as I raise the spoon, who dismisses my warning
that it's a strictly acquired taste…
And who likes it, wants more, a woman
Sito would have approved of ("Never trust a woman,"
Sito said, "who doesn't love food"). And I feed her
some *kibbeh*, and she likes that too, her hair
the color of ginger ale and spilling
over one bare shoulder (her trademark,
regardless of the temperature: dress straps, bra straps,
nightgown flannel – they all fall down).

Later, when she tries to pick up the check
(her other trademark), I fling dollar bills at her plate
until they become the chef salad of a surrealist,
and the marvelous returns to our fingertips,
like the pine nuts (expensive but worth it)
that I nibble in the name of bountiful women:
all the radiant generous ones, past and present,
who never really needed talismans over their doors
to make you feel lucky. Who were themselves
good luck incarnate, reaching across a table to touch your face.

## TENDERLY

Brutal wind at the end of a brutal year.
Bankruptcies everywhere: businesses, marriages,
public peace and peace of mind. I'm a maintenance man
in coveralls and workboots, I'll forage through the neighborhood
for what sustains. Next stop: the food co-op.
Which means passing first through the urinated air
that shrouds little Saint John's Episcopal Church.
I'm thinking: red peppers from Mexico, olive oil, sourdough.
Maybe even chestnuts from Italy, because 'tis the season,
though the season is ever more grimly expensive.
I'm thinking: skin with the gorgeous gleam of chestnuts.
My spiritual practice is not to walk like a saint
among the derelict, but to zero in on their muzzy eyes
and give back their "Hey, man." At the Yangtze Fish Market
on Mission, a Dahomey chieftain's slaphappy offspring
entered with a cry of "Hey, man!" and all the aproned
tractor-capped countrymen of Lao Tzu took turns grinning back:
"Hey, man!" "Hey, man!" "Wha' chu waant, maan?"

At the co-op I'm thinking: Fujis, Pippins, Granny Smiths.
I'm thinking girlboys with earrings, boygirls with buzzcuts,
soon they'll have to disrobe to distinguish each other.
Maybe that's the point: go tribal, then get coital.
At the body studio on lower Fillmore, along with the splendors
of tattooing and piercing, they have added scarifying
and, yes, branding. For years I thought scarifying
was pronounced *scare*-ifying. My spiritual practice
is to look up the words, pronounce them with clarity,
live them with clarity as best I can. Phenomenon, phenotype,
pheromone. Much of me is an indisputable wonder
of machinery, programmed to serve the laws of gratification
while avoiding excrement on the sidewalk, and the sharp corners
of glass-topped coffee tables, and the automatic

manipulations of those who could do well enough
for themselves, but would prefer to have me save them
the trouble. And I don't mean the pisspoor, either,
working the streets for the price of a burrito.
My program at low rev says there are limits to compassion.
At high rev it says give what you can, but give.
And keep moving: there are circles for us yet to complete.

Last summer outside the Yangtze, not ten steps from the mobbed
bus stop of the New World: a fortyish woman, "negotiating"
with two men, broad daylight, one of her nipples nonchalantly exposed.
And then, three blocks up, opposite the Spanish basilica
of Dolores Street – Street of Sorrows, just a block from
Guerrero, Street of the Warrior – on the grassy, palm-lined
traffic divider: a college student on her back, textbook open,
body more naked than not, the occasional driver honking
for her attention, golden-brown vision overlooked by
the chalky Virgin set in her stone niche across the street,
oblivious to the smooth bare legs, one propped on the other,
dangle of sandal, glisten of skin. I thought: My God,
I'd love to conjugate your bones – tibia, patella, fibula.
My spiritual practice is to praise the body, not bury it.
In basketball the white boys say: Good hands, soft touch.
The black boys say: Push it, go to the hole, penetrate,
elevate. My team had it all going – rebound, outlet, fast break –
we were unstoppable, dynasty for a day, and then their center
threw his ogre arm at my launch to the hoop. I hit
the hardwood hard. Took four stitches above the eye. Came back
the next week and started drilling from the outside.
My program says adjust, adapt, all is rhythm.
That summer we'd remind each other – keep cool, stay
in the flow – and our most fluid teamwork we'd call

"Zen ball." The co-op cashiers, weighing and pricing,
quick with the fingers, punching the numbers, still manage

to banter with each other and their customers of choice.
Mine, though, is quiet, phlegmatic. She wears a thin ring at the outside
edge of one brow, not far from my sports scar.
I ask her why there, and she murmurs of a time
she can't go back to. She says: I know too much now.
I'm thinking: thin gold in a circle near the eye –
it's a vision thing. A song comes over the sound system:
forgiveness – the need to have, the way to get it,
the emptiness that follows after its visit. The pale
evening sky, depending on your point of view, is a lovely lavender,
sliver of a moon hinting at brighter things to come;
or the pale evening sky is simply too pale, too dry
for this time of year. Our programs say precipitation:
rain, snow, the headlong rush into amorous engagement,
mammalian warmth. Sour-sweet chutney, basmati rice,
I'm thinking: the Hindu figures at Khajuraho, sculptured
stone, bolder than flesh, voluptuaries going at it, level
upon level of ecstasy incarnate, the sensual body as temple.
I'm thinking: breasts with the supple weight of water,
the eyes circled in black like significant days on the calendar.
A calendar that makes no distinction between a moment
and a millennium. I'm thinking: is it really the Dark Ages
doubled? I'm thinking: I wish to hell I'd stop thinking…

My spiritual practice is to walk: up the steep hill, past
the plane trees that used to lean for my sake into infinity.
To walk up the hill where Being itself waited for me
with the warmest eyes, the softest hands, and to know again
what I knew then: in the untold, untellable history
of everything that ever lived, this was my moment.
My self and the one who was another form of my self,
for whom I was another form – this was our moment together.
After all the privileged, the destitute, the celebrated and the obscure
who had lived their exquisite chance, their fortuitous coming-together
out of all the possible disparities – after all the lovers before us,

it was our turn now… To walk up the hill and see the plane trees
still leaning, and know this life, this latest moment,
this being here which someday won't be, is still mine…

Climb a hill like that without pausing and soon enough
you're coming down the other side: nebula of the next neighborhood,
windows framed with festive bulbs, and strung in some
of the smaller trees, little blinkers like lightning bugs.
The wind's died down, and up floats a wisp of a Christmas hymn –
carolers, making their rounds. Outside the taqueria,
a different show: a chubby young woman in a wheelchair;
a couple of glitzy, long-lashed, miniskirted cross-dressers;
and an unofficial "doorman," long raggedy coat, no hat,
jingling a paper cup for coins. But tonight's top billing
goes to a newcomer, an older musician, his baseball cap
stitched with a big red "A" that's crowned with a yellow halo:
the Angels have fans even in this godforsaken town.
On a glossy black recorder he's playing – with perfect
soulful phrasing – the classic ballad, "Tenderly."
I'm thinking: Eric Dolphy would be proud. I'm thinking:
give the man paper money, give him his due, though money
is only a symbol of what he deserves, what none of us
can do without. The wheelchair woman gets some too
but not as much; she's only there to take, and mere need
doesn't inspire what my spiritual practice calls prayer,
which is not so much an asking that the emptiness be filled
as it is itself a filling of the emptiness.

At the produce stand near my street, an old woman
with native eyes, native hands, is working through
the imported peppers. Checking the color, the bruises,
trying to arrive at what she can live with. I'm thinking:
Aunt Rose. I have got to write her. A woman who says,
I hate winter – maybe it's old age. A woman I have never
thought of as old. Six weeks after her husband died, companion

for more than fifty years, she stood one evening at the stove
and heard him walk through the door, and very clearly
pronounce her name. They call this the "season of peace,"
but it's no different from any other season: peace comes at will –
miraculous apparition – and goes the same, and in between
our work goes on. When I get home to my glossy black altar
of a piano, I'll figure out "Tenderly." I'll float the notes
back into the void that issued them, and I'll do it in the name
of all the people and places, dead and living, we think of
as our daily bread. And now, on the step by my front gate,
someone has left – by accident or design – a plastic-wrapped
deli sandwich, replete with pickle, on a paper plate. I'm thinking:
Who knew I'd be so hungry this late in the day? I'm thinking:

# I FORGOT

Something I was going to say and now I can't remember.
"It must have been a lie," says the Lithuanian plumber.
"You Americans. You are always lying."

\*

This obsession to shape the world to our specifications.
(Frazzled between summit meetings, fast approaching
deadline, she called from the hotel before sunup.
"The world here might not last the week.
I might not last the week.
But you're free, Tomás, aren't you.")

\*

Jogging home after midnight down the country road
because nobody would pick me up,
I kept the water tower in sight.
The mantra of the moment: *Not much farther, not much farther.*
And the more I ran the more I seemed to be running in place.

\*

Takeo brushed one of the ideograms for my name.
Translation from the Chinese: "emptiness."
"What I mean," he said, "is the word the sages use
when they refer to fulfillment of desire."

\*

This desperation always to do something.
(The bumper sticker exhorting ACTION
below a couple of dings and a shattered brake light.)

*

The jetty stretched into the bay and then
curled in on itself: a cue
to some order I couldn't apprehend
but which had to exist.
(This insistence always to see more
than what is there, to transform
what's there into what's desired.)

*


Across a small table at I Fratelli,
someone who with a single remark
justified my existence: "You bring me back
to what I know. With you, I remember."

*


Evening meditation, the eyes close
with relief. Let no one begrudge me
these few minutes of peacemaking...
And when the eyes open: the rays of our local star
define the desk, the density of the wood,
its bulk, its undulant grain.
What was alive in the tree still lives in these planes,
a profound pulse, swelling
from heartwood to sternum...
(That's not a desk, that's an organ!)

*


I forgot: in the lulls between "events,"
in the undistinguished interstices – to be receptive.

That's as significant as anything.
(Walking past the pitched roofs out in the avenues
in alternating shadow and light, shadow
and light, I thought: Ah,
now I remember...)

This was the kind of day you had hoped you'd wake to.
A day for certain powers to work their spell.
Not gods or ghosts, not the sixth order
of angels. Not spirits, exactly.
More like spirit itself, an essence in the air
you could almost inhale, could taste almost.
Outside the red-canopied restaurant
a gust of ginger-garlic sauce
hit you with the redolence of sex
carried away on the fingertips –
and suddenly winter gave up the ghost,
your body was back to being a fascinated animal,
it could wander far and wide, well
into evening if it wanted to.
And it wanted to. It went on
to take as a practical joke
the wild plum blossoms of balmy February,
which from a distance you'd swear
were branches of snow. Other look-alikes
from the world of the lost almost stopped you,
crossing the intersection as you crossed
but heading the other way (as they had to,
because for them this "spring day"
was not an official one). But you fended off
the impulse to follow them back
to an underworld you know too well,
where what appears to have form and substance
disappears the moment you try to hold it.
You looked down instead, someone whose eyes
are used to the ground, and there
in the sidewalk: your initials,
inscribed along the hard way
you travel day and night, alone

and with others. A good omen
here in the concrete, in the only world
you still have the power to call your own.

LITTLE SONG

*Want.    Not want.*
*Want.    Not want.*

Each day, every moment,
a two-part invention

composed of desire
and its relinquishment.

## JOY

When it comes back to teach you
or you come back to learn
how half alive you've been,
how your own ignorance and arrogance
have kept you deprived –
when it comes back to you
or you yourself return,
joy is simple, unassuming.
Red tulips on their green stems.
Early spring vegetables, bright in the pan.
The primary colors of a child's painting,
the first lessons, all over again.

And if you can sit in a little arboretum
not far from the beach, not far from the restless
drivers on the access road, and one dark hawk
suspended midair like some sleight of hand –
sit on a simple bench, down the path
from the herb garden and the gorgeous
flanks of horses, the wood slats bleached by sun,
the ironwork painted the color of grass, and notice
how the shrine to the Enlightened One is set
back into the shrubs like one of them,
and know you've come here to take your place
whether in the scheme of things or out of it –
isn't it enough at last to want nothing
but this? A few moments of unadorned order
without effort or explanation. Each moment
only itself. Ever changing. And everlasting.

## "IN THE EVENING WE SHALL BE EXAMINED ON LOVE"
*— St. John of the Cross*

And it won't be multiple choice,
though some of us would prefer it that way.
Neither will it be essay, which tempts us to run on
when we should be sticking to the point, if not together.
In the evening there shall be implications
our fear will change to complications. No cheating,
we'll be told, and we'll try to figure the cost of being true
to ourselves. In the evening when the sky has turned
that certain blue, blue of exam books, blue of no more
daily evasions, we shall climb the hill as the light empties
and park our tired bodies on a bench above the city
and try to fill in the blanks. And we won't be tested
like defendants on trial, cross-examined
till one of us breaks down, guilty as charged. No,
in the evening, after the day has refused to testify,
we shall be examined on love like students
who don't even recall signing up for the course
and now must take their orals, forced to speak for once
from the heart and not off the top of their heads.
And when the evening is over and it's late,
the student body asleep, even the great teachers
retired for the night, we shall stay up
and run back over the questions, each in our own way:
what's true, what's false, what unknown quantity
will balance the equation, what it would mean years from now
to look back and know
we did not fail.

ABOUT THE AUTHOR

Thomas Centolella was born and raised in upstate New York, where his poetry won awards at Syracuse University and the State University of New York at Buffalo. He was a Stegner Fellow at Stanford University and has taught at U.C. Berkeley, at College of Marin, and in the California Poets in the Schools Program. Centolella has been a resident of northern California for many years; he lives in San Francisco.

BOOK DESIGN and composition by John D. Berry,
using Aldus PageMaker 5.0 and an Apple Macintosh iivx.
The type is Adobe Garamond, designed by Robert Slimbach
in 1989. The roman of Adobe Garamond is based directly on
Claude Garamond's 16th-century types, rather than on Jean
Jannon's 17th-century imitations as most of the 20th-century
"Garamond" revivals have been. The italic is based on italic
types cut by Garamond's contemporary, Robert Granjon.
*Printed by McNaughton & Gunn.*